Bettendorf Public Library
Information Center

THE WINTER LIFE OF SHOOTING STARS

Poems by Diane Frank

BLUE LIGHT PRESS

COPYRIGHT 1999
BY DIANE FRANK.
All rights reserved.

BOOK DESIGN
Shepley Hansen
Natalie Hansen

COVER ART
John Gregorin

PROOFREADING
Penny Minkler
Caree Connet

ISBN: 1-886361-06-1

BLUE LIGHT PRESS
P.O. Box 642
Fairfield, Iowa 52556

ACKNOWLEDGEMENTS

"Window of Poppies" was nominated by
The MacGuffin for the 1998 Pushcart Prize.

"In the Japanese Tea Garden" was nominated by
The Briar Cliff Review for the 1998 Pushcart Prize.

I want to thank the following magazines and
anthologies in which some of these poems were
previously published or accepted for publication:
*Voices on the Landscape: Contemporary Iowa Poets,
The MacGuffin, The Briar Cliff Review, The Contemporary
Review, The Midwest Quarterly, The Urbanite, Voices
International, Eclipsed Moon Coins: Twenty-Six Visionary
Poets, Rattle, OnTheBus, Adagio Press Broadsides,
Museweek, The Iowa Source, In the Theatre of the Breathing
Earth, The Fairfield Weekly Reader,* and *Orbiting Entrances.*

Special thanks to Alan James Mayer, Terry Brennan,
Diane Averill, Viktor Tichy, Rustin Larson,
Meg Fitz-Randolph, John Stimson, Judy Liese,
and the Tuesday Night Poets.

CONTENTS

Window of Poppies 1
Parachute 4
Angel of Eros 6
Hieroglyph 8
Dancing at Old Threshers' 11
Planting Flowers in the Intuitive Garden 13
Olive Street 15
Philharmonic Rehearsal 17
Woman in a Sarcophagus 20
The Winter Life of Shooting Stars 21
Black and White Photograph 27
I Remember the Wooden Horses 30
Moonlight Sonata 33
Beyond the Walls 36
Resurrection 38
Broken Angel 41
North Country 43
Angel above the Landscape of Your Breathing 46
Walking with Rilke to Rodin's Animal Garden 48
Love in the Ice Storm 51
Night Language 53
The Gate 55
The Secret Gravity of Toes 57

Somewhere Inside I Am Burning 60

The Witch in the Snow Mirror 63

The Yoga of the Impossible 66

In the Voices of the Birds 70

Painting Psanky 73

After My Mother has a Near-Death Experience
    and Comes Back 76

I Call It the Big Dipper but the Man Looked like a Bear . 79

Suicide of Light 81

The Spark in the Shadow 83

Flying Girl on a Train 85

Shattered 87

Gypsy Honeymoon 88

Riding to Kambiz 89

Valentine's Day 91

In the Japanese Tea Garden 93

Shaman in Chicago 95

Driving Back from Galena 96

Waltz 101

Dancing in your Shirt 103

THE WINTER LIFE

OF SHOOTING STARS

Window of Poppies

You walk to the abandoned farmhouse
knee deep in the stalks
of last summer's flowers.
It's early spring
and the deep red petals of oriental poppies
are blooming around your ankles —
a color that endures
even after the haystack burns.
This morning, there was a total
eclipse of the sun,
but now the light is coming back.

Above the rattled wood of the porch
and long grey boards decaying into embers
from too much summer rain,
a high cathedral window
stretches its thin blue glass
up to an early afternoon sky
fluttering with geese flying north.

The window seems almost out of place
above the Iowa prairie grass
and the pig farm over the ridge.
It seems more like a poppy than a window,
something too delicate
for the harsh seasons of a land
too far away from the river
where calves are born.
The edge of the sky
is tinted like the poppies
that bloom every spring
but only for a week.

Maybe the farmhouse
was built by an immigrant family
who lost most of their money
in huge Atlantic waves
as they crossed the ocean.
In the new country
they kept bees and sold sweet honey
until their fingers grew wild
with flowers.

The farmhouses of their neighbors
were large, wide-planked, and white,
but they wanted to build their house differently.
They wanted the highest window
to be an altar to
the geometry of snow.
They wanted to build an open
cathedral to the moon.

Or maybe it was a vision
that came in a farm woman's dream,
and her husband loved her so much
he had to build it exactly the way she saw.
And when he cut the wild shape of their love
into the wall
like a shrine of poppies,
he rode a dappled horse in the moonlight
to the only glass blower in Dubuque
who could roll the glass for his window
as thin as a dream.
He tinted it with a tiny song
of aqua hummingbirds
to protect his lover's hands.

The night he finished the window
the full light of the moon
was streaming through the humid air.
The farmer moved their mattress
off the thick fretwork of their iron bed
into a frame of moonlight,
and the way they loved each other
was a mystery in the eye
of a newborn child.

An hour before dawn the next morning,
the cow who ate the shadows in their garden
birthed her calf
on the soft red petals of poppies.
They named the heifer
"Window Full of Moonlight."
Maybe her mother's milk had the secret
of the way back home.

Parachute

I am crawling through a parachute. It's a tunnel of gauze or silk or ripstop, with Persephone pushing my knees. I am blindfolded with a green silk scarf. Or maybe it's purple. Isadora's dancers or dragonflies push my body into distortions. I am wild inside gauze. Spinning inside air. Crawling in the dark towards a flicker of light. It's a mystery covered by a cocoon while meteor showers explode over my shoulders.

There aren't any instructions, and I'm surrounded by ripstop. I'm free falling from the air with prayer flags drifting around my ankles. Floating in the dark. Yellow and black stripes of light and shadow drift across my feet. Banded bees are trying to tell me stories, but all I hear is a buzzing in my ears. I am rolling down a long green hill a long time ago. I am picking a wild bouquet of poppies for my second grade teacher.

I am walking the high beams of new houses abandoned by carpenters of the late afternoon. The last farm stopped giving pumpkins last October, but this is a good place to collect discarded nails with my eight-year-old friends. The beams are an open theatre, and the shadows tell us stories. We have borrowed our mothers' scarves, and we are teaching the bees how to dance.

My lover and I are dancing barefoot after midnight. We are both covered with oil inside a steam of jasmine flowers. I skate counterclockwise over his body before the second hand stops. We might be in Kyoto or Tel Aviv, but the walls are now a blur. My heart is shaking, or maybe it is the walls.

The tunnel is streaming with gauze as I crawl in the semi-dark. The bees are humming softly on the other side of the parachute. The tone is silk or translucent, and floating. It's a new kind of music that I refused to listen to before. The bees say the erotic is in the shadows, and nobody can love without the wound. They tell me we all need to be pierced to know the mystery.

I am dancing inside a parachute, and suddenly I don't know how to fall. I am high above a ferris wheel of strangers, a thousand paper cranes after the bomb explodes at Hiroshima. The sake, still warm from the heat of your hands, is spilling across the table while you paint on my back with ink-covered fingers.

There is someone whose collarbone I see in my dreams. He sings to me in bass or tenor overtones in a familiar language. I can almost hear him breathing while poppies grow through the cracks in the slate path. I meet him in the tunnels between the pyramids.

Angel of Eros

Montreal thunderstorm.
Jazz ripping through water
in the minor key of the
late afternoon.

He's been avoiding her
in the shiver of the current
of the stream that flows north
through his land,
in the deer tracks buried
under the fence
before it falls down in a blizzard,
in the cows that escaped two weeks ago
from his neighbor's farm.
But now his scent is melting
through her hair.

He is greedy for her words,
but she keeps them hidden.

She tells him to keep the white room empty.
The shelves he built so carefully
are not for his books.
It's a place where the future vibrates
in holographic messages,
a tunnel from the hieroglyphs
underground.

She runs her fingers along his collarbone,
shaving bark.
The music evaporates
like oak leaves dissolving underwater.

In the open room
the humid air settles
like the density of a desire
that is still invisible.
The only furniture
is the atonal harmony
of a cello weaving through water.
The only voice
is the finger that ripples
down his spine and whispers
keep the room empty.

Hieroglyph

Maybe the Fisher King
was bleeding from his thigh
because he wanted to be a woman,
a woman in moon time,
a waterfall of rose petals
dripping from his knees.

You spend your evenings
watching science fiction
as if the layered images on your eyes
could fill with light and somehow
crack like a robin's egg
to remember the interstellar
colors and shapes of time.

You are stranded in fields of lichens
between the earth and fire
in the petals of tiger lilies.
Shoulder high in prairie grass,
you run barefoot around the reservoir
the blonde girls swim in
after midnight.

Elderberry blossoms
snow on your forehead
as you dream of the landing cones
of light from flying saucers,
your ears finely tuned
to messages that spiral
from a distant home.

South of town
the tinny water tower
stretches its fat finger
to the moon.
Beneath your fluttering eyelids,
the reflection of stars
ripples like a slow tide
in a land you've left behind.

Turtles swim
to a white shadow floating
beneath the pond.
Maybe it is a swan
or maybe a woman,
her back patterned with lichens
and oak leaves with long fingers.

She whispers:
    "Out of loss is created
       great mysteries."

Embracing all of her slippery
hesitations,
you emerge from a tortoise shell
and slip between the rocks.

Her eyes pull you beyond memory
into whispers, into the shadows
of an ancient home
where even the writing of hieroglyphs
was forbidden.

You smooth your fingers
along the leafy stems
of her dancer's legs,
lifting her beyond
the amethyst curtains of the sky,
peeling her words
like thick green petals
of an artichoke.

She offers you water in her hands,
later in the husk of a coconut.
But after midnight
the mammal heat releases
into the light between your bodies,
into the vaporous trail
of shooting stars.

Dancing at Old Threshers'

Tangerine sunset floats low on the horizon.
The moon is orbiting around your hat.

I dance with you between rows
of early September corn,
your Amish beard a field of uncut hay.

I haven't memorized the map
of the constellations, but your eyes
are burning. The landscape of your muscles
ripples under your white muslin shirt.

You turn me two hands round
as the Great Bear rises in the sky
above your left shoulder.

There's a secret beneath my gingham apron,
a shower of falling stars
as we dance around the fire
kicking up the ground made hard
by late summer rain.

We orbit around the shapes
of our forefathers' stories —
a galaxy of seasons changing,
the stars a blur,
woodsmoke and wisdom whirling.

As we circle around each other,
the bear wakes up from his dreaming,
hears the tinny music
of hammered dulcimer floating south.

He pulls corn out of the husks
and you open your mouth.

The moon cracks like a pumpkin.

The sparks brush your skin
like a woman with turquoise beads,
tan muscular arms
and the secrets of your shoulders.

I am the goose shadow dreaming
of the day the universe began,
singing the music of the next creation.

Planting Flowers in the Intuitive Garden

I didn't plan where to put the irises.
The bulbs went in like a snowfall,
and two seasons later
when squawking geese shadows
flew south across the moon,
poppy seeds scattered where they fell.

As the tangled roots of warmer weather
push their way to the surface of the field,
daffodils collide with tulips.
Blueberries twist their branches
around rose petals
like a dancer who has stretched so far
beyond her natural shape
that the form has to break.
I dance in the garden at night
with pink lace climbing my ankles
and my toes bruised like blueberries.

Every day I add another flower —
columbines surprising the lattices on the porch,
shasta daisies with double rows of petals
wild as ostrich feathers or snow,
nasturtiums with edible blossoms.
Summer comes in a flood, but the wind
is still breathing with dahlias
curling their leaves toward unknown colors.

I want to make love in the intuitive garden,
with peonies bent to the ground
by thunderstorms.

I want to dance in a gallery of angels
surrounded by wildflowers
and a pasture of goats and sleep.
Every day I add another flower
like the petaled surprise of love.
Every day the magenta blood of wild berries
stains my fingers and my cheeks.

Olive Street

For Margueritte Struble

There was something about the quality of light
that morning we walked by stucco houses
at the edge of the school yard,
boys playing with sticks
at the edge of the creek in Cedar Falls
and the field you used to play in.

Something about the light on your face
as you pointed to the last window
of the prairie house where you used to sleep
now whitewashed over the pink,
the tennis courts
where you couldn't defeat your older brother,
the wide faces of sunflowers in the garden
growing like beanstalks
or dreams inside a genie's ear,
and the clearing in the woods
where you practiced kissing girls
on the back of your hand.

Your Latin teacher is 88 years old
when you knock on her door
thirty years later on Olive Street.
The angular bones in her hand shake softly
as she strains to hear your words
through thickened membranes
inside her ears.

But as she pours tea with flowers
into three cups of her finest china,
she remembers the dreams
of a young boy from Iowa
who wanted to live in France.

In her memories
you will always be fourteen years old,
but she almost lets you hug her.

There is something about the silver
scarf with red flowers
draped around her neck,
the gold barrette with open roses
pulling the white tangle of her hair
away from the open softness of her face,
and her silver voice
searching for the late morning sunlight.

Look, her hands are shaking with music.
Her voice is trilling
like a field of hummingbirds.
Words are spinning around her fingers
like bees flying towards a secret
in the humid dusty yellow
center of an iris.

A smile is spreading like watercolors
over the parchment skin of her face
almost transparent as the pages
of the Latin books you used to read.
Something delicate ripples in the light
reflecting from her hands.
As the late afternoon light
shatters on the swing set
beside the Quonset shack in the yard,
something is glowing through
rose petals.

Philharmonic Rehearsal

The Italian philosopher called us angels
with only one wing.
He said we could learn to fly
by embracing one another.
But what about the spider
eating the mayfly
in the frame of my bedroom window?

After I fall asleep
I am back in New York City
at a rehearsal
of the New York Philharmonic.
My grandmother walks out of her grave,
puts on a black satin dress
dangerously off the shoulders,
and her opera glasses.
She kisses Leonard Bernstein
on the forehead.

A friend hands me a cello.
After twenty years
I will learn to play again.
It needs to be repaired,
but she reassures me that music
will spiral out of the wood
with a new bridge and new strings.
She tells me about a man who lives in Brooklyn
who can bring out the angel
in anything made of wood and silver.

In the late afternoon
I am in a neighborhood of strangers
with the cello over my shoulder
and my other hand on the strap
where the wing should be.

A man I know partially
in dark and light shadings
of a puzzle that doesn't fit together
geometrically
is walking ahead aloof,
holding a crippled child
on his shoulder.

His parents are trying to
resurrect a forest on the slopes of Oregon.
They cover themselves with lichens
and roll on moss
below pines that will disappear
secretly, at night.

I try to tell him about my grandmother,
but the sidewalk shakes below
the rumble of an elevated railway.
He vibrates into the sound
and disappears into elongated shadows
of the late afternoon.

Meanwhile, the rest of us
are beginning to discover
the magic of Arabian horses.

I shift into the city,
into the desert,
into the crescendo of the symphony
just before the conductor
hesitates.

Arabian horses
run through the orchestra
in a path between the tympanies
and the trombones.
Then they leave
by the emergency exit
like a line of streakers
at a high school football game,
a wild parade of angels
or a waterfall of shooting stars.

Woman in a Sarcophagus

If there had been an ocean
inside the pyramids,
it would have looked like this:

Arms crossed
suspended between cliffs
a woman is floating on a rock,
below her
the sea unraveling.

She doesn't know
the time of moon or morning.
She can't see
the reflection of her face
inside cumulus clouds,
underwater lilies laced with shadows.

At sunrise the light ripples
so a woman can take form
inside of salt,
sliding through ocean
waves, into the phosphorescence
of a dolphin's wandering.

This is the gift
the waters offer you,
and the currents are deep enough
for the singular journey
of your shoulder blade,
a shark's fin
forming from the embryo
like particles of a photograph.

You complete the story.

The Winter Life of Shooting Stars

*When you wrestle with an angel
and try to overcome her
is when you get wounded.*
—Dorit Har

1.

When winter came
I ran out of your words.
I couldn't even find them dreaming.
Your words became a genetic code
hidden inside sunflowers
and shooting stars.

Above the northern border
your voice spread like a supernova,
a shower of first snow,
but I was too far south
to pick up the frequency.

Strangers called you on the telephone,
and your words tumbled like water,
tumbled naked
on the rocks, silver
inside streams of falling stars.

You wanted to give yourself
only to yourself or distant strangers,
a Bodhisattva of the radio.
Now you belong to everyone,
especially your voice.

2.

We are riding on a train through Northern Ireland.
We travel through a field of dinosaur bones
and prehistoric war horses.

A woman I don't know
is singing in the post office,
her voice sweet as a sunflower,
all of us waiting for messages
or sending paper airplanes
to places we can't see,
as if people in other countries
could love us more
than we love ourselves.

As if her voice
could make the snow melt
before its time.

A comet arcs below
the Big Dipper.
Through my telescope
the particles distort and blur,
focus and separate.

You are still in Canada
hiking on trails that cross
a frozen river,
lost inside a room of Persian
carpets.

Locked in my own silence,
I have become a hologram
naked
in a mountain spring
surrounded by silver stones.

3.

After the first snow,
I dance to the music of
a violinist who knows how to travel
between stars
with a partner who can't see
my home.

His glasses form a border
around his face,
a fence around the meteor showers,
a cage for the wildness.

I am lost inside a crowded room.
Someone whose voice I only heard once
in a field of lavender
slides in behind me,
pulls me to his chest,
and I melt into his voice.

His wrists are a compass.

His hands trace the definition
of muscles under silk.
Under white dancer's tights,
a suggestion of soft petals.
But I don't know where this dance
is leading.

4.

The clock is a night light.
At two o'clock in the morning
it is twenty years ago.

I am teaching children how to swim
inside the belly of a whale
with a glass window.
Every two weeks
we send off helium balloons
with postcards tied to a string.

Now it is Tuesday.
I am watching a sky full of
red blue green and yellow
balloons
disappear into the late afternoon.
Maybe I'll get a postcard from the Pleiades.

Here is the message:
"If you find me,
   tell me where I'm from
       and mail me back."

5.

The snow falls under a street lamp
in a city where I haven't lived
for twenty years.
Or is the sand
shifting in layers around
the pyramid walls?

Sometimes I think that life is a singing lesson.
Hitting the right note is intuitive
and mysterious.

I haven't heard your name,
but I see you in hologram —
the tendril of your collarbone,
the neon blue ice trail
of a shooting star.

Black and White Photograph

His house is hidden in the woods
by a thicket of walnut trees.
The only sign of life
two white buckets
leaning together like lovers
in the left corner of the
photograph.

He speaks to me in f-stops:
the sink full of copper pots
and bottles of antique glass,
the wood-burning stove
lit by a match from the 1800's,
the bicycle
leaning under the bedroom window
with handlebars that already
have become vines.

He says, "The subtle shades
are what brings out the luminosity."

Everything is light and shadow…
the edges of late afternoon sunlight
inside bottles distracting
the vertical lines of his windows,
the shadows of elderberry
leaves waving above the violets
when sunlight comes from the backs of things.

He says, "In the camera's eye,
you are looking at the back of your own retina.
You are swimming in a world of light."

The low range brings the shadows luminous...
a clutter of branches under his window
with fingers reaching for blackberries
under a ripple of hand-rolled glass.
The high range highlights only.
Shadows fall into the valley
of unfinished dreams.

There are images I can't capture:
the scent of deer musk,
the printer's muscled forearms,
and the slanted light on the printing press
folding shadows.
The pile of his grandmother's dishes,
and the silver goblets
waiting for hands.

He closes the bathroom door,
draws a thick curtain over the window,
fills the lion's paw tub
with trays of Kodak developer,
stop bath,
finishing rinse to erase
the edges of water.

In the dark
we watch the images appear...
pure metallic silver
blooming like sunflowers.

I would like to adjust my life
to the shutter speeds of a camera…
slower subject with the sky deeply blue,
cottony puffs of thunderclouds
hanging low in the eastern sky
above the slats on the porch swing,
and the dancer with luminous hands
still touching the sparrow's wing.

Everything is light and shadow…
rivers inside a bee's wing,
and the braided girl leading a goat
through waving petals of sunflowers,
the whole world blooming, everything
lit from within.

I Remember the Wooden Horses

I don't remember my father's hands
on the beach at Coney Island
when I was two years old,
or the way he cleaned the sand
off the red rubber ball
he tossed to the sun
before he caught it for me.
I don't remember where we found the sand dollar
that was twice as big as my hand.

I don't remember the iron bars
of the jungle gym
at the park in Irvington
where my mother took me.
There is only a photograph
with the face of a tiny friend
dissolving like the shards of a dream,
with blossoms of clematis
waving like a veil
on top of the orange berry bush.

I remember the wooden merry-go-round
with yellow, red and green
boards to stand on
and a wild wind in my hair.
I remember the swings with heads like horses,
but I don't remember the way my mother
pushed me towards the sky.

I don't remember crawling around
my grandmother's double bed

while she was dying of cancer.
My mother tells me I was the only one
who made her smile.
I can't remember her face,
but it seems a lot of weight for a two-year-old,
crow's wings hovering on my shoulders.

I don't remember the garnet necklace
wrapped around her throat,
even though I wear it now.
I was too young to notice
the lines of pain growing around my mother's eyes
like rivers of ink,
my tiny hand linked to her fingers,
and the hands that carried her
reaching for an ultimate peace
beyond the wooden horses.

A tall woman in a tangerine skirt
in front of a room of pillows
talks about radical honesty.
How is it possible
when the memories that shaped me
are as elusive as
the tinny laughter of a tambourine?
How is it possible
when the memory of your touch
is light floating through stained glass
on the way to the moon?

It's the ripple of the muscles
in my father's arms
before he swings at the softball
in the diamond the neighbors made
on the other side of the vacant lot.
It's a secret in the closet
of the house that only flashes
from time to time
in a disappearing universe —
in cracks between the splinters
of the wooden horses.

Moonlight Sonata

*The untuned piano is the legacy
from my family. It was my mother's way
of saying no to the only desire
she could refuse long distance.*

My mother asks me to visit so that she can show me heirloom silver, jade beads, and silk kimonos from my grandmother's trip to Japan. As I fly east of the silo, I press my face against airplane glass. My vision opens to the control tower at the airport, the metallic roundness of floating architectonics, and the long row of lights leaning into rain clouds. A slow journey into the evaporation of boundaries held by different points of view.

As I hurl through the stratosphere in a long metal tube with wings, I drift back into the Japanese temple fire of the massage last night. Soft willows brush up my spine in Sumi-e ink tones, and his muscles are a magnificent God sculpture. Now it blurs into a silo filled with alfalfa, and sweet Williams blooming at the edge of my grandmother's barn. Or a message inside the long neck of a Modigliani Aphrodite in earth tones.

Time bends counterclockwise as I leap through a hoop of cumulus clouds. I am surrounded by bronze sculpture, see my arms ripple out of stone, watch the new clay drying on long rows of shelves by the Western Wall. The sculptor I dance with shapes the mud he found by the river into the wild bending of lovers. I watch the clay take the shape of muscles under his fingers, and the Goddess he kisses with his shaping tools has my breasts. But he doesn't finish any of these pieces, never takes them to the fire. As the months go by, the sculptures crack inside the wash of light from the bay window.

My mother's arms ripple out of fur as she gathers me into her arms at the airport. She is 66 years old, but her eyes are still hypnotic. As we drive to Paoli's for flowers, fish and flamenco serenade, winter trees slide by the window. My memories crescendo like the Doppler of the semi-truck that crashed into my friend a month ago.

After I fall asleep, I watch a man on a tractor insult my mother. He doesn't know me well enough to speak in front of me this way, but in his mind, I have become invisible. I am picking sweet Williams and trying to forget what I am seeing right now. I think of the words of the sculptor. On the way to the airport he told me, *"You own us. We live for you. Any man who gives you another answer is lying. The answer isn't in asking. It's in owning. All of the cities, the buildings, the sculpture, the art is for you. Marriage destroys that because we get to choose. In reality, it's the other way. You choose."*

I'd love to share this with my mother, but she is already losing her voice. Hummingbirds hide inside the ivy she has so carefully rooted, and she wants to sleep for a thousand years. She forgets to show me the silver, even when I ask. I want her to sit with me by the piano, but she is already too distracted.

I want to play the Moonlight Sonata, but the piano hasn't been tuned for five years. The pads under the hammers are starting to disintegrate, but some of the notes still sound sweet. When I was fourteen years old, this piano was the center of a family feud. My grandmother wanted me to go to Juilliard, but my father said, "Not over my dead body." He thought musicians grow up weird, imbalanced in other parts of their personality, and he didn't want that for me. Nobody ever asked me what I wanted, and I was still too young to let them know. Now, thirty years later, time has settled everything.

But I am rebellious, and I play the sonata anyway, even with the sometimes tinny notes in the treble clef. Once again, I'm being told that everything in front of my eyes isn't real. The sculptor whispering inside my ears is covered with the paint of new beginnings, and I need to recreate my memories again.

Beyond the Walls

I walk into a synagogue in Poland.
It is fifty years ago — before I was born.
The men are in a large
room with white
shawls over their shoulders.
The edges are fringed like sheaves of wheat
or snow falling between branches of olive trees.
The women are in a small room to the side.
It is warm there — like soup.
The light is the color of soft candles.
They invite me into their circle of song.

I am standing outside the Western
Wall of the Temple in Jerusalem.
It is two thousand years ago.
We are carrying sheaves of wheat
over our shoulders
as an offering to God.
We are a human river of white robes
and sandals, with flecks of wheat falling
into the sun around our feet,
like a prophecy raining from a cumulus
cloud filled with voices.
We enter the gate to the outer
wall and dance with our wheat,
shaking it in all six directions.
But the mystery in the center is closed.

There is fighting in front of David's Tower,
outside the Jaffa Gate.
Too many soldiers from I don't know where.

Suddenly I am floating
in the air above the Temple walls.
I am higher than the crows
who lay their eggs above the Temple walls,
higher than the doves who hover
over the Mediterranean Sea.
I am filled with love and light,
and I can speak to God directly
as though he is my closest friend.
Suddenly I know the mystery
inside the Holy of Holies.

Resurrection

1.

Bands of fuchsia and lavender
fall behind the bare
edges of winter trees.

You give me a stone you found
on the steps leading down
to a concentration camp
in Austria —
an amulet stolen
from the water of dying.

The stone breathes in my hand.
It speaks to me
in a river of memories
of every hand
who held and let go
of a blue heart beating —
the wind of unfinished lives,
a child's skull cracked on stone.

I don't know if the memories
are what I hear
or my own.

My breath comes back
like ice crystals around the moon.

This is the way
we let go of everything.
This is the way
we forgive the world.

2.

A thin ray of sunlight
shatters inside a crystal angel
floating in my window
before it diffuses
into the colors of morning.

I am happy just to be breathing.

I gather silver fish
in a wooden bucket.
My bare feet
curl around the rocks
as they redirect the water.

I braid my hair
in the mirror of the river.

My ancestors laugh at me
in the mirror of
a beaded photo frame.

I draw patterns on my arms
while the sun evaporates the water —
beads of sunlight dancing.

This is the way
I want to dance
when I'm ninety.

3.

Now I hear voices in the wind —
the heavy steps of my father
and mother's shivering hands
by the window.

Faces crying in the stone
paths leading up from the river
ankle deep in snow.

I remember the suffocation
in the cattle cars,
the stone soap they gave us
just before the light went out.

We floated up
and God was singing to me
at the edge of a lavender field —
a soft melody twisting around
the bones of my ancestors.

I surrendered my breath.
I let go of the brass candles
as blackbirds
floated in and out
of the flames.

Broken Angel

There's a broken wing of an angel on my bedroom floor. It hardened into glass at six o'clock in the morning, splintered all over the room, and one of the thin glass bones pierced the bottom of my foot — the part I need to dance.

The Kabbalah says that we are all created with a spark of the divine. Our thoughts, dreams, emotions, even our bodies hover around the spark, spinning like planets around an elliptical orbit. Then, before we are born, they harden into shells around the fire. The wild language of our dreams, the fire of our emotions, the tears of our transitions, the kinesthetic mystery of our skin are all gifts from the spark — a minotaur's maze designed to open the way back.

When I was three years old, I invented a language for the planet I insisted I was from. It was a place where children rode tricycles upside down, and words spun counterclockwise inside the colors of dreams. Or maybe it was something I remembered. My best friend spoke this language too. It was a secret we shared, and the neighbors didn't understand why we left our tricycles leaning on the handlebars by the telephone pole at the corner. Or why we wove the reeds of tiger lilies into the chain link fence around her yard. Nobody understood the words of the songs we sang to one another — a chant which has echoed too often through my life.

I keep a box of matches to light my Sabbath candles. Red and green letters say, "Rosebud. Strike on box. Contains 32 damp proof matches. Keep away from children. Close before striking." At midnight I'm spinning so fast that I don't know where to fall, but something inside me is afraid to burn.

Angels speak to me in familiar voices. "Keep on walking in the dark. Sleep in an open field of tiger lilies. It will get warm in a few months. Dragonflies will tell you their secrets. Feel the alone. Love the empty place inside of you until it starts to hum and glow. That's the ripple where you'll feel your future. We're always guiding you. Our love burns like your candles. Trust the sparks to tell you where you need to grow."

Every transition is blind, and when the rope bridge crosses a river you can't see, you have to feel your way with your hands. I think of calling 911 at three o'clock in the morning, but the voice at the other end says, "We're too busy. Why don't you call one of your friends?"

One of my dance partners lifts me over his shoulders and takes me down three flights of stairs. As he carries me, I think of a crystal necklace I bought in a small antique shop on a narrow street by Lincoln Cathedral twenty years ago when I was hiking around England and Wales. It's probably lost in the bottom of the chest of a woman who isn't a friend anymore. Or maybe it shattered like an angel in an abandoned stained glass window. But as she falls to the floor, she whispers, "Sometimes gifts from the angels come in splinters."

I can't see my future, but I feel like I'm creating myself every day — even if my foot is still bleeding. I let my hair spin until it's wild, and circle around whoever is in front of me, gypsy style. Part of me is still afraid, and the path I walk in the dark is full of mud that sticks between my painted toes. But as I am walking, the cows push their brown heads softly into mine and suck my fingers. They pull off my scarf and fill me with the soft scent of morning, even if the spark is still hiding.

North Country

I've been flooding myself all week
with flowers, aromas and herbs
to smoke you out of my house.
I light candles inside a cocoon
which becomes a circle of glass,
but it doesn't get rid of the wound
around my mouth. You hover
around the silent place where I dream,
a banana slug pushing the translucent
line between sleep and morning,
so yellow.

You cancel my trip to Toronto.
It isn't the right time, you say,
for me to enter your
world of wood and windows,
the ephemeral city of sidewalks,
the river of hidden faces, desire
searching for God in the form of a human body,
the cries and whispers of unrequited longing
in a single voice.

On the telephone close to midnight
we talk about the way language creates reality.
Take your own words seriously.
It's a code, you say. I'm searching
for the invisible thread to the future
as it falls apart like the echo
of a spider's web.
In a single phone call,
you have become a memory,
a disembodied voice.

After I fall asleep
the banana slug attacks my garden.
You are the next incarnation of a bleached blonde
driving around an unpaved midwestern town
in a blue Plymouth station wagon
with a customized license plate that says "TAXI."
We are two trains colliding south
on the Canadian border.

What is a border anyway?
An invisible finger across a line
where a lake becomes two different countries.
We divide our lives into whispers
as you travel north into an eclipse of the moon.
But part of you remains further south
in the sky over a wheat field
electrons leaking from the aurora borealis,
until I find your voice
in the center of a meteor shower.

I walk with you into a wood filled with hummingbirds,
a field of sunflowers rising over your shoulders.
We lie down there, but I come out with
splinters of bark in my hand.
I want to connect the rivers between our countries,
to bathe in the currents of the stream
that runs through the border of your land.

When I put my hand on your chest,
I begin to bleed.
Your beard is a porcupine.

When you kiss me, your quills
wound my mouth.

In another country
I gather baskets of peppermint and basil
from my garden. To see you
I have to cross an invisible line
over a wheat field or a lake.

I put your pillow in a box
and mail it back to Canada.
The place in my scapula
that aches when I'm lonely
hovers around your mouth.

I sleep with the animal, the chest of fur.
I sleep inside your scars, as well as mine.
I feel your hidden longing through the corded
tunnel to my solar plexus.
The quills of your scars
scrape against my face.

Angel above the Landscape of Your Breathing

The cows lick my fingers before the snow falls.
I push into the center of the herd,
a heavy cloud of
brown cow faces licking me
in a wide field starting to freeze.

I travel back from the heat and shadows,
away from the wild urban
rhythm of tap dancers on construction beams
to prairie fields that are too open,
wheat fields covered with snow.

Beyond the snow's exhale
I feel the heat of your body,
the landscape of your breathing,
your thoughts a percussive rhythm
on an empty stage.
You can fill it
with origami boxes or wings,
or something you pull
out of your chest
through a wall of flames.

We dance in feathered shadows
of longing.
In asymmetrical landscapes
you pull me through the fire
to the edge of your
heartbeat.

The tap dancers
are wild on the steel arms
of construction beams
angled up to the sky.
They become shadows
in the high beam
of headlights forming a tunnel
to the Pleiades,
the shapes of their dancing
waving in the steam
of a cloud.

I wrestle with you
like Jacob's angel
knowing that you could lift me
or pull the ligaments in my thigh.

Sometimes I still have trouble walking.

Walking with Rilke to Rodin's Animal Garden

The light inside the peonies
is an open trail to the hidden light in me.
As we walk below balconies
of narrow, winding streets
that disappear into unexpected
corners and alleys
the way life does at times,
I tear the mouths of petals
as if they could reveal the secret of atoms.

We are walking to the zoo
to see parrots, snakes and panthers
with our words as deeply
as Rodin knows them with his hands.
One of my teachers told me I see the world this way —
finding my way through the maze
of love and cottonwood
by touch
and saving my eyes for a deeper reality.

But your world goes further than that —
a language I could only hope to discover and earn
after long conversations with the Duino Angels,
walking through the panther's shadow
on the narrow silk ribbons
of a swallowtail's wing,
or curling inside the crab nebula
until the sleep of the universe ends.

I live at the edge of my elbows
pushing out to the last

dolphin swimming at the border
of a watery, green horizon,
inching my way through
the last curtain of ocean glass.
I embrace the statue of Apollo,
his back, his fingertips
until I re-invent his eyes.

You have always been the one
to encourage me to dive straight into
the green wave that's already ten feet over my head.
You have already walked on this water,
and you of all people know
with the certainty of the mud in the panther's footsteps
that even when I have forgotten how to breathe,
I will tumble into the currents
that lead the angels home.

You ask me to open my eyes underwater.
You tell me I will find emeralds
in the eyes of the rainbow trout
who is swimming with me.

You ask me to walk down unfamiliar trails
in the dark of a new moon.
You tell me to leave my matches
on the kitchen table
and feel the way with my hands.
You invite me to taste the fruit
the sculptor gives with clay covered fingers —
even though I don't know if it's mango or poison.

You whisper, "Take the longest path up the mountain,
and if the sun doesn't give you enough time,
spend the night with your eyes wide open,
shivering with white deer between cottonwood trees."

You are the one who tells me that there is nothing
so frightening or terrible that it doesn't need my love.
You tell me that every ending is a beginning.
You tell me it's fine not to know the answer to anything,
and that the shape of the unknown
is where the new is born —
the hidden womb inside the seed
of a mango or a poppy.

Together, we're building
a living totem of
sunflowers, angels, panthers
and words that will gestate
with the patience of an angel
in the bark that scrapes my hands.

LOVE IN THE ICE STORM

Two days after the ice storm,
shards of oak trees
heaped around the yard,
five thick branches of the hundred-year-old elm
split off, crossed,
crashed against my house.
The Russian olive
heavy with eighteen hours of ice
cocooning the branches,
pulling them to the snow's gravity,
and the sculptor in my yard
weeping over the devastation
of a chainsaw that made a mistake
in the aftermath of the ice
and fire of an argument
he had with his wife this morning.

You say love is like these trees
splintered and shaking in the echo
of the ice wind
with indigo balls of lightning
bouncing from tree to tree
in the eleven o'clock sky.
You say that even if the sculptor
made a mistake,
new branches will grow back
to fill the hole in the sky
too large now for the moon.
You say love
has to survive these storms
and you can't resist
the muscled arms of nature —
you have to bend or crack.

As you say this, the sculptor
leans against the elm,
thick inside the padding
of his tan winter down.
He says, "I could have saved that branch
if we didn't argue,
if I didn't need somewhere inside
to make your yard
like the splinters of her words
over the ice chunks
I threw back."

In Hans Christian Andersen
they would say
it's the fatal kiss of the Ice Princess.
We circle dancing like gypsies
eye to deep eye
but never allowed to touch
while rivers of ice crack below our feet.
I've been climbing the highest branches
to ice music
after midnight. When I
shimmy down the wide bark of the oak
in satin dancing shoes, you
catch me as I fall.

Night Language

When you throw a glass of champagne in someone's face,
don't apologize.
Its soft aroma is full of the sharp-edged words
you were afraid to say last week
and every request he didn't listen to —
even in the feathers of your sleep.
The bubbles are the explosion
of the softness of your arm
that has been pulled away from his chest
while you were dreaming.
And the broken glass in the corner of the room
is fragments of an argument
you would have had next Tuesday.

He says he needs time without me
to find himself. He tells me
the sweetness of the way we love each other
has folded an echo over the drumbeat
of his hidden longings,
and he can't hear his own voice anymore.
But every night when he dreams,
he floats over my bed in his feather body.
I have almost forgotten the voice of my own dreams.
I can't hear the breathing of tiny birds
in a nest of peacock feathers.
My skin has forgotten the heat
in the musical curve
of the small of his back,
but when I wake up in the morning,
a shadow on my chest is breathing
in the shape of his hand.

At night, hidden voices come and tell me
that time is a holding pattern
in the helicopter shape
of an anopheles mosquito.
I follow a trail of blue wings
into the jungle,
an archeologist's hammer in my hand.
Smooth black stones are tumbling
along the edges of a river
with the promise of trilobite fossils inside.
But the mosquitoes tell me
not to crack the rocks open until later.
They tell me to put the stones under my pillow
until the feathers float in my bed
through the morning.

The Gate

For Sandie Kopff
"The world is recreated every morning."

I saw you dancing in harem pants
   by yourself with rubies
      just below the hollow of your throat.

You've been forced out of your house
   and now I see you worshiping
      in trees, singing the highest notes
         in a forest of bare branches.

Maybe it's the withdrawal of hormones,
   those molecules of endorphins
      meant to keep you bonded for life.
He sleeps with his new lover
   on the other side of the branches
      in a bed I thought was mine.

You climb the wrought iron fence
   that surrounds the peach trees in your yard.
Your legs stretch under the cold
   as your muscles flex like dancers
      and begin
         to feel their shape again.

Maybe your breasts are rosebuds now
   waiting for the thaw.

The ice whispers
   feel the alone.
Shiver
   in your spine
      until you glow.

Sometimes the days come too slowly,
   the slanted winter light
      crashing against the ice.

You sleep inside the snow
   with your head leaning softly
      towards the sunrise.

The singing comes from underneath.

It's the opening to a field of lavender
   as you walk through a cedar gate
      painted white with the roses of longing.

Once again, you're learning how to see
   in a light where everything is new.

The Secret Gravity of Toes

for Pablo Neruda

Since we stopped walking together a few weeks ago, I've been staring at other people's feet, even at times when my ankles feel too weak to carry me across the dance floor. The secret of this obsession is the way you have loved my feet for almost two years. When I look at my feet on my pillow or take them in my hands, they are peach-colored birds, soft as mangoes, reaching to be touched, still singing to you.

I love my two bridges of bone, the angular collection of protrusions and direction, my pathway over the dirt and stones we walk on every day, on the oasis that lifts us so sweetly we don't even realize we are flying around the sun. The earth is the dancer who holds me while I arabesque, the muscular partner who guides me so softly I don't even feel the gravity of his arms.

My feet carried me 18,000 feet into the sky on mountain trails in the Himalayas. They kept climbing while I was learning how to breathe in air so thin that the totems I fight at lower altitudes dissolved. They kept lifting me higher while the life I used to live dismantled itself and never came back. They chanted to the sunrise while the last star in the sky sprayed its light just above the peak of Gangapurna.

My feet have danced inside mirrored walls and windows in San Francisco. They've leapt like twin gazelles above the waterfall of *Ein Gedi*, the winding stairways of Jaffa, and silk-covered Bedouin markets in Jerusalem. They've run with me through long rows of decaying corn in the Iowa field of dreams. And they lifted themselves into your hands two winters ago in another wild adventure through the minotaur's maze of attempting to stay warm.

Now they're back on my pillow again, reflecting themselves from a round mirror in the satin light of a *piña colada* candle, alone. They are dragonflies orbiting in a mating dance, a secret gravity in the moonlight.

Why do you want my feet to be a memory? The massage oil you adored them with is still next to my bed. Maybe someone can explain this to me. You're lucky right now — you have family and friends to pull you out of the shadows of your longing. I don't belong to anyone.

I've been dancing at night in concentric circles. I am the gypsy with the ring of opium poppies around my long, dark hair. I am surrounded by a circle of other women's children.

An Israeli woman I dance with says that I am a yellow rose — exotic, lovely, but not the kind that fits in a bouquet on anyone's kitchen table. She says I am too unusual to be the finch in most people's tulip garden.

Right now my garden is full of artichokes. But when I try to eat them, my throat closes up. They are the spiked green memory of the love I used to put on your table. Maybe their fleshy petals are a collection of frog's toes from a fairy tale where nobody turned into a prince. Your petaled napkin is still on my table. I'm still talking to you, like a blind dancer balancing herself on top of a cedar chair. The rose petal sauce I would have prepared for your birthday orbits my kitchen like an undiscovered planet and flies back into the pages of a book. My words echo red around the musky scent of blossoms.

At the Jewish Film Festival in San Francisco last summer, the screenwriter from New York said that Jewish women in films always lose their man. We were sitting in rows at the Castro Theatre before the organ prelude to the eight o'clock show. She gave examples: Baby in "Dirty Dancing," Barbra Streisand in "Funny Girl," and Bette Midler in "Beaches," who ends up with her best friend's daughter but not the man. I've been trying to write myself a different story.

So now that I'm dancing again, I'm watching feet. Rachel has long black hair and eyes as dark as the sky around the moon, but her feet are twisted branches that fell to the bottom of a forest in a thunderstorm. Sarah's second toe is longer than the others, and her middle toe is wide and flat — a secret that only her sandals reveal. And you are still bonded by heavy cords to a woman with thick ankles. Her feet are swollen like yeasted bread. The dream you haven't stopped chasing is pigeon-toed.

I wonder if bent toes are a message from the underworld of the body. Or maybe an inner voice saying things that you wouldn't say out loud. I wonder if my own feet are comets out of orbit that will somehow find their way back to the gravity of hands.

Somewhere Inside I Am Burning

You reach for me in the darkness.
A black hole in an immensely expanding sky.
A shadow before the Big Bang.
A canvas that your naked hands have not begun to paint upon.

At the banks of the Ganges River
you see a funeral pyre
with a woman bound to the sticks.
She is still alive and she is burning.

Somewhere inside I am burning
even though the Siberian irises in my garden
are blooming white and deeply purple
inside the curves of their vulva petals.
Even though the ants are breaking apart
the buds of the peonies
with fuchsia petals and heart perfume.

And who is that naked person
falling out of concentric circles
of the humid summer sun?
Or is it winter?
My back is arched into
the transparent vapor of a passion
that drifts between angels, between clouds,
between constellations in a tilting sky.
Or maybe it's just a season.

Maybe the circles of sunlight
are a code for an implosion
in the center of the Crab Nebula.

Is that your face in the center of the vortex,
or a stone? Is it fear
falling out of sunspots
or aurora borealis?
Are the rivulets of salt water on a path
flowing back to your eyes?
Are they your eyes or my own?

Somewhere inside I am burning.
Salamanders slither up from the river,
fly like doves into my hands,
into the shadows,
into the flowers of my body,
and the snake shadow wrapped around your left leg.
I call to the columbines,
the Great Bear, the constellations —
embryos on the tree of light.

And a sound comes that is mysterious,
each time pronounced differently
and heard in bird voices
or the cadence of a waterfall.

In the copper of a Tibetan bowl,
you see a woman burning
on a funeral pyre
on the banks of the Ganges River
inside a vision of mud and flame.
She is still alive,
the wood splintering her back,
and you ask me not to burn.

I hear your voice
as a breath
of peony petaled light
inside a nightingale.

Everything is speaking to me —
the birds, the waterfall,
the voice inside the fire.

The Witch in the Snow Mirror

At midnight our footprints disappeared
like a lunar eclipse in a forest
that offers no way back.
I was holding the mittened hand of my brother
as we wandered further into the dark.
It was so late that even our dreams had no beginnings.

The witch's house was round as the full moon,
lit with flames escaping from an oven
where skeletons burn.
But my brother was hungry,
lured by the sweetness of gumdrops
as big as his hands.

As he filled his hunger with sweet pink bites,
he fell through a tunnel of leaves
into a golden cage in the witch's kitchen.
Then she walked into the forest,
blinding the moonlight with a candle.
She held up a mirror where snow was always falling.
My brother was caught there.
She said if I wanted to talk to him,
I'd have to come inside.

As I followed her, the leaves turned dark
inside my footsteps. Her eyes,
clouded by shadows, could only see
by looking through the silver.
I became her step-daughter,
cooking wild chickens in a pot
with myrrh and feathers.

When the witch put her hands inside the silver
of my brother's cage,
he gave her bones instead of fingers.
But his bones were hidden now.
At night, as he walked through the labyrinth of sleep,
all of the doors and windows were closed.

I walked into the forest to search for
wild mushrooms, lichens, poison roots.
I wandered into the snow mirror,
chasing the footprints of an old woman's shadow.
Inside the mirror she stalked me,
a white deer running
through a forest of eucalyptus trees.

She became a raven, a crow, a shadow,
until the beating of her wings
cracked the mirror.
The clouds in her eyes began to snow.
The cobras around her ankles
unwrapped themselves,
and she became suddenly beautiful.
Then she disappeared.

When I walk into her house now,
I feel like I own the forest.
Not in the way she tried to,
but since I shattered the mirror she held for me,
the wildness of trees and birds is inside me now.
My brother has become the moon,
and my long, dark hair falls down to my knees,
filled with wildflowers.

The lichen soup I used to cook
has become a waterfall.
And the mirror I use
to see myself
is my own open eyes.

The Yoga of the Impossible

We might be traveling cross country,
but that's possible.

We fill the back seat of the car
with antiques to be traded
in Pennsylvania, New Hampshire, and Maine.

We navigate from the Midwest to New England
by the flowers — foxglove and chicory
on the banks of the highway,
tiger lilies and Queen Anne's lace
at the edges of the ponds,
at night *The Egyptian Book of the Dead*
floating through our dreams.

In the kitchen of my grandmother's farmhouse,
I massage the asphalt and fatigue
out of your legs and your shoulders.
Below the Big Dipper and the Pole Star,
fireflies are blinking possibilities.

Swans float under the full moon
in the pond on the far side
of the sloping cornfield —
the pond with the belly of mud
and the heat of the inner tubes
I used to swim in as a child.

Night shadows of branches etch your shoulders
in a pattern you long to discover,
perhaps in the attic of an antique shop,
or a message in hieroglyphs
from an Egyptian dream.

Silently, we shift positions —
the gestures of the Yoga of the Impossible.

I wonder if you will touch me
in a way you haven't known before
but you say it's impossible.
You say it's because of a wound in my foot,
edges charred
around the scar of a cave.

We continue traveling northeast
below the Bear's left shoulder.
Across the Tappan Zee Bridge,
two exits on the Cross Westchester Expressway
to the Sawmill River North.

Black-eyed Susans and white pines
at the edges of the horizon,
larch pine forests rippling the mountains,
aspen leaves shimmering silver.

In Maine we drink tea in your mother's kitchen.
Her kitchen is a cocoon
woven with gifts from flea markets,
beeswax candles, grandmother china,
and Eskimo sculptures of long necked swans,
totem families,
shamans in flight —
sculptures carved from stones
you can hold in your hand.

She asks you about your life
as you tell her,
"What I had in mind isn't quite possible."

In the late afternoon,
we hike down the long slope to the cove,
launch a boat your father built
in the estuary water.
I walk with your mother,
carrying plates
and a basket of ripe pears,
wild vetch and sorrel blooming at our ankles.
We build a fire of beach wood
on a shoulder of garnet rocks
and mussel shells.

Later we climb over boulders
below hedges of wild roses.
I watch waves swell and break for hours
before I close my eyes.
I am the wild goose shadow
etched into glaciers,
wide Atlantic waves crashing
into a high tide.

The shining ones
from *The Egyptian Book of the Dead*
curl through unfinished dreams
from moonlit waves
to the back tunnels of your mother's home.

I melt into a transformation
from fractiles
into extended textured plains
of rock heather, sorrel, mussels,
mother-of-pearl,
sea lavender.

You float through the ivy melody
of a mountain violin
as I climb the pyramid tunnels
of an Egyptian dream.
I am the beating of a heron's wing,
the footprints of a cormorant
dissolving in your hand.

You are looking for a hand
as familiar as the antique cups
in your mother's kitchen
as we dream of shark fins,
shoulder blades,
two feathers spiraling between
light and shadow
only fingertips away.
But that would be possible.

In the Voices of the Birds

What I most remember about Christopher
is the way he knew the names
of all the birds
at dawn
by their songs.

His cornsilk blond hair
blue overalls, no shirt,
the strength of his shoulders
and the way we stayed awake all night.

There was light in his touch
between the birds.
They flew in and out
of his fingers,
and birds outside our window —
a window we couldn't
open again that way.

We met when we could after that,
in Iowa, Switzerland, San Francisco,
in borrowed cabins on two different oceans.
You took me to my brother's wedding
in a red pickup truck,
made fun of the priest and my brother's future
mother-in-law,
which you claimed permission to do
because you were Catholic.

I remember the way you hurt me,
what you said,
and the sentence I typed on your
portable Smith Corona in Nantucket
before I left
for the last time.

It was November,
with a light dusting of snow
over the sand.
The pebbles on the beach
hid their messages.

On separate sides of the continent
we listened to different oceans
and slammed our lives shut —
you in Brooklyn Heights
with your two-year-old son
on your shoulder,
me in San Francisco
climbing the long hill
to 24th Street.

Twelve years later,
holding your first book of poems
in my hands, I am
hungry for memories,
hungry for every word,
hungry for any hint of a message
where I might find myself.

In the inscription, you write:
"There are histories
in this book you may
be familiar with, because
you were there."

I am not the arms
where you will rest your head
when you're eighty years old,
but I always hear you
in the voices of the birds.

Painting Psanky

for Suzanne Niedermeyer
Psanky are Ukrainian Easter Eggs

The postman delivers fantasies
stones from Indonesia
liniment for my muscles
unexpected dreams.

It's Valentine's Day
and my mother is moving to Florida,
the Jerusalem of the West,
following the trail of her father's
bones.

Suzanne and I are gathering eggs,
waiting for winter to disappear.
The sky is unrelenting
as the snowscape.
The field meets the sky
like an eggshell
at a cold white edge,
but it doesn't crack.

A man who pretends he is Rilke
steams up my windows
and disappears.
He locks his bicycle
behind a rose bush laced with snow,
takes a train to San Francisco
with his back towards the East.

A month later
I find the key under a shower
of frozen rose petals.

Two weeks before my birthday
I drive into a snowstorm
to hear a cellist from Sweden
to search for a silk kimono
to see Kabuki woodcuts from Japan.

As the snow falls
I drift to the desert in New Mexico.
Joy is singing there
and I want to sing with her.
She is thunder, an *arroyo*,
a kachina who weaves the sky
with long blue parrot feathers
through her hair,
as the wind paints Hopi tiles for the cathedral
ceiling of the mountains,
names the seas and craters of the moon.

Inside the snow storm,
Suzanne and I are painting psanky,
etching patterns with wax
inside an ecliptic of constellations,
filling the orbiting sky
with eight-pointed stars
against banded colors,
dyeing the eggs and the edges
of our fingers.

Roosters come into the living room
with clucking and white tail feathers.
Suzanne is playing Mozart as the postman delivers
a letter from a bicycle,
a postcard from my mother,
wild geese flying through the rusted
shadow of the moon.

Inside the crust of cold
I have become a triangle, a snowflake,
a heron on a journey.
My dreams are full of flamingos;
they predict an increase in wealth.
Stars on eggs spin into snow storms,
meteor showers, constellations,
a train taking me home to San Francisco,
a weekend inside blue feathers
dancing to the North.

I scrape the wax off the dots
of a small egg in my hand.
The stars are a thousand kisses
spinning in the dark
inside a milk bottle
from the postman.

After My Mother has a Near-Death Experience and Comes Back

I decided not to resist the change of seasons this year,
to let the shorter days come all the way inside me,
the brown drifting leaves
and the cold.

My mother wants to be released
like these maple leaves
ripe and red
from strong trees falling.

It's harder to build an altar for someone
who is still alive.
She sleeps curled
inside a heron's nest,
a separate soul
who has to make her own decision.

My mother's voice
is weaving through silver
branches of winter trees,
the braids of her childhood
thick and brown
like soil, like bark.

This is the voice
that sang me lullabies,
the photograph of her childhood
inside three strands of
seed and potato
pearls.

I light candles.

I touch her braids,
thick, brown, cut off
in the drawer where she kept her scarves
next to my grandmother's opera glasses,
beaded purses from the first part
of this century,
and other silky things
to play with.

They say at times of transition,
heaven is closer to earth
door of death
door of birth and renewal
a house filled
with cotton wool and angels.

At the solstice
I walk outside to the silver
trees thick with moonlight
and the wind says,
let go.

Love her, bless her
let her go.

I lift my arms
to the ice, the wind, the Pleiades.

Three winters after the ice storm
the tops of the branches
have grown back,
slender, new and green against the sky.
They cover the open space

where the sliver moon
shines through.

Lacework of moon
and winter leaves,
a fluted sky,
the night horizon circling
an altar of stones,
blue comet flying
through the strings of light.

Viola wind
crashes through high
piano notes. Winter storm
flows into solo
violin
forest full of trees
circled around me.

Silver flute
flies through strings
around a circle of
ocean glass
into a snowy egret's
mouth.

My mother is still singing to me
the way a cello
speaks from the f-holes.

The memories and the desires
release a lacework of leaves
on the brown earth.

I Call It the Big Dipper
but the Man Looked like a Bear

Meteor showers
in a time warp
halfway between San Francisco
and Tel Aviv.
August in the hills
just East of here
halfway up the scent of
eucalyptus.

Sitting on the warm blue
metal of your car,
emotions a spray of August
meteor showers,
the sky purple, scattered
midnight.

And the constellation
above your left shoulder.
I call it the Big Dipper.
You say *Dov,* the Bear.
And sex, you say, is like
eating or sleeping,
a natural part of life,
something people do
who feel close to one
another.

But I am a woman,
and I might fall
in love with you,
something people do
who feel close to one
another.

And how
do I find my way back
from this cave of *Ya'alim*,
weaving my way
through scarves and clay pots
in a Bedouin market,
drunk with the scent of
eucalyptus?

The constellations
carousel
and you are the
magic horse.

Love is a constellation
between two languages,
an amethyst
banded around my smallest
finger, weaving through
scarves embedded with gems,
an ocean of
cumin, cucumbers, apricots
in a Bedouin market.

In your voice
something about water,
the Dead Sea.

Suicide of Light

I knew that something was wrong
when you threw your bicycle in front of a train.
You wanted to see if there would be anything left
after the metal cracked
and what shape it would be in —
an attempted suicide
but only in metal and red paint.
You were laughing from the sidelines
and taking notes
on the shape of your emotions
while the train was screaming.

The last time we made love
you were screaming like a train.
I don't know when the snow fell that night,
or why you had to walk away.

Sometimes you have to love against all odds,
even if it seems crazy
and your friends think your emotions
need a trip to the zoo
in a faraway city.
Sometimes you have to write messages
in letters shaped like flames
in the ice on your rearview mirror.

The angels say
you are an apple peel —
some sweetness there to be sure
but not the whole fruit.
They say you are cookie dough

in the shape of a raw star
that needs to be baked —
a star that will get stuck in my throat
and choke me.

I say you are a supernova
exploding without control
in a galaxy moving away from you.
You are needles of rain
new and falling on
my shoulders.

You are the eclipsed light
that refused to shine on my shoulders
after I held your rain —
a vortex
trying to find its way
back home
after the light becomes empty.

The Spark in the Shadow

You promised to clean the spider webs from my ceiling.
Six months later, the windshield wipers
on my car are still broken,
but the crack in the universe
is where the light comes in.

We come back from a week in the Valley of the Saints,
and you walk out of my door the next morning
still locked in the embrace
of a dark woman in white silk
with a diamond in her nose.

I stand at the edge of alfalfa,
the field waving in heated summer
air after a thunderstorm.
My thoughts follow the wide arc of the sun
to mountain slopes
that lift like dancers from the ocean
in a land that used to be my home.

Dragonflies hover
over the memory of my grandmother's pond
as my face ripples in the water.
I swim with eels and catfish,
my eyes open underwater
as the shadow of my hands
disintegrates
into a green blur.

At night, I rock on the porch swing
under a sliver moon.

I had wanted larger windows,
expanding circles of poppies,
Siberian irises at the edge of a koi pond,
stone lanterns
with a light I could rely on.

Now I'm walking back into the forest,
leaving behind a trail
of thin metallic hearts,
the light around my body
reflecting a swarm
of hummingbirds.

I'm walking
in the amber light
like a porcupine
moving through a code of wooden nails
with both of my hands
on fire.

Flying Girl on a Train

Like a tornado that is simultaneously
frightening and lovely,
she leaves town without saying goodbye to anyone —
a marginal voice already beyond the limits
of her vocal cords.

She mails postcards to every man
whose eyes have ever brushed her shoulders,
saying, "I won't forgive you,
even if you bring me flowers.
It's already too late for that."

The list of her father's wrongs
is etched in cactus
into the center of her palm.

At night she paints tattoos of violets
on her shoulders,
runs naked with foxes
to an open field
where no one
can hear her screaming.

Later she dreams of a Greyhound bus
pulling away from the grocery store
in a small town in Texas,
with the eyes of a ten-year-old
pressed to the glass
on the other side of the rain.

She is so angry
that nobody can touch her.
But sometimes when life is too quiet
she sings to the foxes,
her voice full of
violets, rain and cactus,
poppies, tattoos,
tornados.

Shattered

On the seat of my sky blue car
linen dyed Ishtar blue.
The grey blue of the narrow road
winding through the desert like
a silver snake
wanting to be runway.
And the sky
at the edge of the ocean
wanting to fill itself with
cumulus dolphins.

The speed of a sky blue car
wanting to float
in a sky dyed Ishtar blue.
Cumulus clouds like dolphins at
the edge of a tidal wave.
And the glass on the pavement
after the baseball bat
shining like Egyptian jewels.

There must be something violent
in me, something shining
Ishtar blue.
If there was an impulse in me
to shatter anything
with a blue stone or a boulder,
it cracked last night.
It fell out of the window
in pieces
like a pile of Egyptian jewels.
That space is empty now.

Gypsy Honeymoon

First your voice came.
Then the photograph.

I am meeting you from the inside out.

Even before I see you,
I might be stroking the fine
hair of your forearms with my words,
running the soft edges of my hands
along your ankles,
or kissing the whisper of your collarbone.

I know that bone —
I saw it in a dream.

If I open the lighthouse,
can you stand the intensity
of silver fish swimming to the moon?

Right now it is midnight.
Two lovers are kissing on top of a stone wall
as their shadows stretch across a gypsy garden.
They walk through wild asparagus,
lupines, opium poppies,
mountain trails of wild irises.

Rhododendron petals
float to their bare
feet over stones.

It is only moments before I see you.

Right now we are picking wild blackberries.
Right now we are the happiest people in the world.

Riding to Kambiz

He says, "Beware of the dark man
on the dark horse,
even if it's me.
Especially if it's me."

On the way to Iowa City
he leans over and says, "This isn't a date."
Then he brushes his hand across my cheek
and puts on music that
sends me beyond the edges of the
pink sun falling.

We watch erotic movies
and don't touch each other.
He sits on his hands while the blonde
movie star exposes her pear-shaped breasts.
He is galloping to the moon
astride the undulating s-curve
of wooden horses.

I open the door to the barn,
climb a tower of alfalfa,
crowd into a ring of heifers.
They suck on my fingers
while a team of Arabian horses
runs into the horizon.

He's trying to change my paradigm.
I'm falling off the horse
while the Apollo Spacelab Team
is orbiting the moon.

And the autumn wind
is blowing north to Canada
carrying the scent of
alfalfa, honeysuckle, cow.

Valentine's Day

You grind your hips
into charcoal
smoky glass.

Your face becomes
ancient Tibetan seer
star nebula
stone mountain.

Or maybe you're just
teasing me
pulling me through a concentric
circle of slow whispers
where I shiver
on the other side of the
fish pond.

Maybe this is a mating dance,
but my fingertips
speak a different language.

The alphabet swirls like gypsy moths
spirals into the neon
of ionospheric storms.

My hands are open
slowly filling with the small
suns of chrysanthemums.

As I trace the calligraphic shapes,
they evaporate like rain on
rose-colored cellophane.

Chocolate doesn't help.
The charcoal ripples on canvas,
leaves an echo of a muscle's
roundness on stone.

Rose petals cover my eyes
as I spin away
from the elliptical orbit
of your touch.

In the Japanese Tea Garden

I can't find the language yet
for these snapshots of friends —
three fish swimming
around the bonsai island in the lagoon,
one golden, one muddy, one silver.
Laura tells me they have been swimming here for fifty years
while the water under the wooden bridges
ripples with light from the other side of the world —
light that has traveled millions of miles
through space.

I see my friends moving in circles of obligation
like plumbing in an old hotel,
a loaf of French bread steaming in the oven.
No, I don't want to take my father shopping.
No, I won't make my mother soup tonight.
You want to float through a maze of expectations,
wind through the arms of a Japanese fern.
You want to be a maple leaf suspended in the air,
by the single thread of a spider
who is now elsewhere.
You want to free your elbows,
roll with the rocks over tumbling water,
but you find yourself spinning around
in a hall of mirrors
when all you can see is the reflection
of your face.

At night the moon is pouring down
the red tile roof
of the pagoda by the fish pond —
chrysanthemum tea filled with light.

A dragonfly from the hands of the Buddha
circles around the thumbprints on my chest.
Soon I'll be flying east again,
crossing the oceans of the moon,
but the Buddha inside the bronze
has left a message on my skin
like the print of yellow leaves
as they disintegrate
on the footpath to a garden of chrysanthemums
that is not my home.

Shaman in Chicago

You meet him dancing.
He impresses you when he lifts you
over his head and turns you
upside down.

You wander into the lightning,
stretch into pilgrimage mountains,
an avalanche of wild geese
flying over the
icefall.

You free his body heat
as he stretches on the sand
in his totem body,
as he wraps you inside
the wild shadows
of his longing.

He has the positions
memorized —
gazelle, zebra, snake,
snow leopard.

In the photograph
his smile is too big.
The shaman, the Taoist scholar
is in the cheekbones.

When the world is too cold,
would you rub whale oil
warmed by a candle
over his muffled breathing?
Would you wash him
when he dies?

Driving Back from Galena

1.

We ran into the shivering morning,
took hands as we tumbled
down the slope
of the trail we were finding
through early November trees,
carefully avoiding
roots and sticker branches.

I lie on my back
below branches
of a deciduous forest.
You hover above me
a deer, a crow
a shivering
inside.

2.

I follow a gypsy moth
that traces the edge
of the Mississippi River south,
the sky wide,
the clouds rippled.

Crossing the bridge over the Apple River,
a road that leads us in separate directions
for the next four weeks,
the edges of my body are transparent.

Sometimes I'm singing.
Sometimes I'm listening inside.

3.

Crossing the Mississippi
the hills after the harvest
curve like your shoulders.

The beauty of Iowa is hay-colored,
unpretentious —
the peeling paint of a farmhouse,
the lacework of branches
at the edge of a wheat field.

At the side of the road
a cow,
a fallow pasture,
the bones of a tree.

4.

In the late afternoon,
my body is a gazelle
as you lift me
above the waterfall.

I am an Egyptian dancer,
a double belly roll

that starts at the ankles
and ripples to my forehead,
a wave of the hips
that rolls through my shoulders.

In your dreams,
the women are on trapezes.
A shard of glass
is buried
between your shoulders.
You are spinning,
losing it.

5.

I sing in a high, clear voice
in an open field,
my cadence a waterfall,
the sun a tangerine.

A deer
as brown as mud
leaps through the alfalfa
just before sunset.

That is the omen.
He doesn't speak to me,
but I invite him to run
through my dreams.

6.

A man with an Amish beard
stares at me
over the pebbles of his
cheekbones. He leans
against the walls of his
covered carriage
from the 19th century,
his horses pulling him slowly
into the sunset.

The edges of the thistles
are transparent.

The mud deer
runs into my dreams
through a meadow of red clover.
You stare at me
through the lake
inside his eyes.

7.

I filter the sunset
through water saturated with
petals of violets
inside a teacup
of hand-blown glass.

The glass fuses splinters
I have pulled from your
shoulders.

There is a violet
hidden inside me,
the center soft as moonlight,
the edges rippled
around the constellations.
But the petals won't open yet,
even when I am naked
under the trees.

We sleep together in the forest,
our dreams a thistle trail.
A gypsy moth holds the lantern
over an echo of blackberries,
as you brush my petals open
with your mouth.

Waltz

The comet discovers a blue path
over your shoulder,
spinning through outer space
above the wood porch railing.

We are whirling to the harmonies of
"Star of County Down,"
your arm in the midheaven
of my back, holding
burgundy velvet.
A violin is weaving through
the flute,
but your eyes hold me to
a deeper melody.

Around the borders of
my seeing, your hair
curls into a halo of memory.
Maybe it is the full moon
or the thunderclouds gathering
out of season
over the rolling Wisconsin
cow pastures
predicting tomorrow's snow.

As we circle around each other,
the wind swirls over
the red barn
next to the 19th century
school house,
a terrifying beauty
that will blow the walls apart.

If I invite you into my house,
I know you would take the time
to find the trilobites
and the seashell fossils,
to see how the curve of the cello
fits my leg.
I'd watch you fold the prayers
you have almost forgotten
into the saffron wrapped around
the bare feet of the Buddha.

And in your eyes
I might find the blue imprint
of a comet,
a message from a planet
near the Pleiades
etched by a ten-year-old
with a switchblade
into your largest finger,
an almost forgotten memory
of the way back home.

Dancing in your Shirt

It's a hot day in February. Unseasonably warm. The sun is heating an April brew of hormones, making everyone think we've had a premature end of winter. It's creating a strange chemistry, hanging out of car windows, chasing miniskirts. Or maybe this is all a big joke.

As I toddle down the road in my white Toyota, I follow a 17-year-old in a red convertible with a white vinyl top. He's tilting down the road in a midwestern farm town that is too lazy to pave its side streets in a linear way. He is dreaming about ribbons leading nowhere, or stretching down to the port from a boat his grandmother took when he was six years old. She was sailing to the Virgin Islands.

The rap beat from his stereo is shaking houses on both sides of the street as he cruises down the road in his long red boat with the top down. It's an African tribal rhythm that he feels in his body but doesn't understand. His car is hot. He's hot. I'm just watching.

I walk into the ballroom where I teach Middle Eastern dance. I borrowed your shirt because my February layers are too hot. I want to orbit like a dervish without steaming. You said I could have anything on the left side of your closet, so I dance inside blue tie-dye with Egyptian bead flowers on my face. Your shirt is a river bleeding out to an ocean in a Cambodian boat filled with jasmine blossoms. A river that bleeds blue blood and dances silver.

I want to feel what it is like to dance inside your shirt. It's a place where you are at your level of mastery — in the zone — and I want to know how that feels in your body. Maybe dancing in your shirt will add an additional layer of tone to my muscles. Maybe I'll be able to turn my partner upside down and hold him over my head.

Or maybe I can dance an invisible *pas de deux* with you, whirling in swan feathers, while a gardenia opens in your hand. Your Russian dancer eyes have traveled back in time, beyond the scimitars. We're dancing in the silent space where every memory is a white rose. Our bodies stretch into a sacred whirling communion. You are orbiting like a planet, into a realm of day and night, where every limitation becomes a gardenia. Where every untraveled love becomes its own peace.

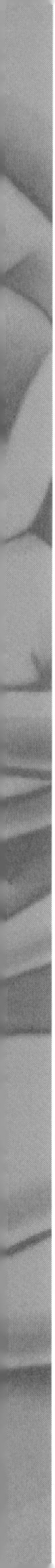